LOVE YOURSELF and KEEP GOING

The Transformation to Greatness

by
KAREN COOMBS

Love Yourself and Keep Going

First Edition: January 2023

ISBN: 978-1-955622-29-5

DEDICATION

Thank you to all the people who have loved me, helped to raise me, helped me throughout my healing process, and always supported me.

Mom, I cannot say how much I love and appreciate you. You are my rock! I became the woman I am today because of you. I know you did everything to ensure that my life was and continues to be filled with love, protection, peace, support, and learning. You have given me the best things in life: your love, time, and care. Your love remains truly unconditional.

Thank you, God, for blessing me with my son, Jaden. You entrusted me with Your child to love, provide for, and protect. I will continue to pray for Your strength and the tools that I need to raise this young man to become the person You created him to be. Jaden, you are the most precious thing in my life. I never thought that I could give this much love to one person. My life has changed for the better because of you.

Thank you, Dad, for everything that you have done for me. I am grateful for your love, guidance, and support. You always make me laugh, even in my darkest moments. Thanks to you, I have learned never to give up.

Faith

Now faith is confidence in what we hope for and assurance about what we do not see. This is what the ancients were commended for. By faith we understand that the universe was formed at God's command, so that what is seen was not made out of what was visible. And without faith it is impossible to please God, because anyone who comes to Him must believe that He exists and that He rewards those who earnestly seek Him.

Hebrews 11:1-3, 6

Perseverance

When you pass through the waters, I will be with you; and when you pass through the rivers, they will not sweep over you. When you walk through the fire, you will not be burned; the flames will not set you ablaze. For I am the Lord Your God, the Holy One of Israel, Your Savior; I give Egypt for your ransom, Cush and Seba in your stead.

Isaiah 43:2-3

CONTENTS

Courage

And we know that in all things God works for the good of those who love him, who have been called according to His purpose.

Romans 8:28

⌇

So do not fear, for I am with you; do not be dismayed, for I am Your God.

Isaiah 41:10

⌇

Therefore I tell you, whatever you ask for in prayer, believe that you have received it, and it will be yours.

Mark 11:24

⌇

But seek first His kingdom and His righteousness, and all these things will be given to you as well.

Matthew 6:33

⌇

If any of you lack wisdom, you should ask God, who gives generously to all without finding fault, and it will be given to you.

James 1:5

⌇

MY PURPOSE REVEALED

A S A LITTLE GIRL, I always dreamed of becoming a teacher. My mother would tell me stories about how I used to play school with my cousins and go out in the front yard to teach the trees. The stories were funny because I would actually punish the trees for giving incorrect answers. My mom would speak about how passionate I was about my lessons at the tender age of 5 years. I was born in Ocho Rios, Jamaica, on December 4, 1979. I cherish the memories I have of my parents before they filed for divorce, which happened when I was 7 years old. Even though my father was not with us all the time because of his line of work, which was to work on a ship in the food and beverage department, I always felt loved in my home. The divorce broke my mom, and even though I was just a child, I felt her pain. I witnessed some of the hardships that she endured as a single mom over the years and promised myself that they would never happen to me. I would make sure that I would be self-reliant and financially stable if my marriage did not work out and I had to provide for my family.

Was I manifesting these assertions for myself and did not know it, or did I truly believe in my mind and heart that I would be strong and have more opportunities than my mom did? My life did not start on a rough path; I did not live a life of hard knocks. As a matter of fact, I came from a middle-class income family in Jamaica. My mom and dad worked full-time jobs and were able to provide a comfortable life for their children. Because my dad traveled all the time, my mom stayed in Jamaica to take care of the family. She even hired a live-in nanny to care for us children when she was at work. Having a live-in nanny was and still is a normal practice for many families in Jamaica. I was happy, and life was good. After the divorce was final, my mom and dad agreed to relocate the family to the United States.

PAVING THE ROAD TO A BRIGHTER FUTURE

AT AGE 12, MY BROTHER and I immigrated to the United States to live with my mom in Chicago, IL. I started Grade 9 in 1993 at Dunbar Vocational High School. I had already been attending St. Hilda's High School in Brown's Town, St. Ann, Jamaica. The education system in Jamaica was adapted from the British system, which starts high school in Grade 7. Everything was foreign to me because I had never visited the United States before. My first winter in Chicago was an eye opener, and my experience living in Chicago was insightful. The 2 years of high school that I had completed in Jamaica gave me the advantage of breezing through the first 2 years at Dunbar. I had to decide whether to study computer science or business during my sophomore year in high school. After deliberating carefully and speaking with my dad, I decided to pursue computer science as my major. I recall my dad telling me that learning about computers was the best way to go because it would pave the way to our future lives. I was on the honor roll from the first year all through high school. Although I graduated with honors, I realized that I was not fully prepared for college.

Deciding which college to attend was stressful, but I chose Illinois State University. I took 1 year off to prepare myself for college by changing my study habits and preparing mentally for this new academic journey. I wanted to save my time and money, so it was imperative to know exactly what I wanted to study before starting college. I thought about my childhood passion to become a teacher, but instead, I decided that I wanted to become a computer programmer. After taking several programming classes, I changed my major to computer information systems. This new major allowed me to take computer classes and be well rounded and informed rather than focus on the one discipline of computers.

Life at college was great. I was happy, doing well in school, and making new friends. I was elated to be on the Dean's List after my first year at Illinois State University. Why does the devil decide to intervene and try to steal your joy when life is going great? My second year of college started with chaos between my mom and dad. They had a significant blowup that placed me in the middle. It was a sad and heartbreaking situation, and it was one of the worst times in my life. At the end of the day, my dad wanted nothing to do with me, leaving me depressed, hurt, confused, and questioning God. I had done nothing wrong, so why was I being punished? I started to skip classes and failed a couple of them. My mom realized how much the situation between her and my dad affected me negatively, so she decided that we should relocate to Naples, FL. The change was exactly what I needed. I enrolled at Florida Gulf Coast University, where I was able to continue studying computer information systems. Toward the end of my junior year, I met a great guy whom I fell in love with after 1 year of dating. We got married in 2005 and welcomed our only child in 2007.

Vision

And the Lord answered me, and said,
Write the vision, and make it plain upon tables,
that He may run that readeth it.

Habakkuk 2:2

⌒⌒⌒

And my God will meet all your needs
according to the riches of His glory in Christ Jesus.

Philippians 4:19

⌒⌒⌒

Ask and it will be given to you;
seek and you will find; knock and the door will be opened to you.
For everyone who asks receives;
the one who seeks finds; and to the one who knocks,
the door will be opened.

Matthew 7:6-7

⌒⌒⌒

Trust in the Lord with all your heart
and lean not on your own understanding;
in all your ways submit to Him,
and He will make your paths straight.

Proverbs 3:5

⌒⌒⌒

EMOTIONAL TRAUMA

I WAS EARNING GOOD MONEY AS a young adult. I moved to Jamaica after my wedding to live with my husband. On our first wedding anniversary, I took a home pregnancy test that turned out to be positive. We were overjoyed as our little bundle of joy grew inside me. We decided that I would go back to Las Vegas to be with my mom for the last 3 months of the pregnancy and to give birth. I gave birth to a healthy, beautiful baby boy on April 23, 2007; he was perfect! I had a supportive and loving husband and a healthy and beautiful child. I felt as if I were on top of the world for several months. I was happy, but unfortunately, the happiness did not last forever. I had to decide whether I would move back to Jamaica to be with my husband and be unemployed for an unforeseeable period or stay in the United States, where I could continue to make good money and go back to school while continuing to apply for jobs in Jamaica. I applied for several positions in Jamaica but had not received any calls to be interviewed. I began to see some red flags in my relationship with my husband that made me worried and fearful. They triggered old memories about what my mom experienced, so I refused to be financially dependent on my husband. In 2008, I decided to stay in the United States, which boiled down to the end my marriage. We continued to live in two different countries, and I knew that having a long-distance marriage was unsustainable. I tried to make the marriage work by relocating from Las Vegas to south Florida. I even purchased a house so that it would be easier for my husband to sell his business, relocate to the United States, and start a new business, but something, or should I say someone, was holding him in Jamaica.

I was in for a rude awakening when my marriage fell apart. Once I learned about his infidelities with several women in Jamaica, I filed for divorce in 2013. I was crushed and broken, and I felt betrayed. I had been faithful all these years, taking care of our child, and not asking for financial assistance from the day that I found out I was pregnant to the time we got divorced. I did not want to become another statistic of a failed marriage and a Black child living in a single-parent home. I always prayed that my family would stay together, but we did not. I started to question God again. The two men in my life whom I had trusted the most hurt me the most. I could not comprehend why these things had happened to me. I started to question my worth, purpose, and future. What is the answer when you have tried it on your own for so long, and the world, people, and loved ones have failed you? God!

TRY GOD

I WAS BAPTIZED IN CHICAGO IN December 2003, but my life did not change significantly after making this commitment to God. Some things that did change included not going out to party as often, wearing different types of clothing, and speaking in different ways, but I was not consistent. It was not until my divorce that I realized that I needed another dip in the water to help me feel whole again. I knew that this was unnecessary, and my pastor spoke with me about my decision, but I wanted to move forward as a personal choice. I needed a support system to help me through the pain, help me to take care of my son, and hold me while I cried and tell me that everything was going to be fine. I was baptized again at a church in south Florida and soon after decided to relocate to Las Vegas to be with my mom.

After moving back to Las Vegas, I decided to start my life over. I wanted to live a purposeful life, so I began to make life changes. I revisited a list of goals that I wanted to accomplish; I had written this list while living in south Florida. One item on the list was that I wanted to earn my master's and doctoral degrees. I had already completed the MBA program at Nova Southeastern University in 2011, so the next educational goal was to obtain a doctoral degree. I created a new plan, which I did not know at that time was a vision board, but I wanted to purchase a second house in 2016, enroll in a doctoral program, get married again, have another child, and become a professor. Yes, I returned to that childhood passion of teaching.

I had no idea how I would return to what I had always wanted to do, but somehow, gaining experience in the information technology sector, coupled with my education and real-life experience, gave me the courage to pursue a doctoral degree. As God would have it, I wrote my letter to Him in December 2015, and He blessed me with a house in April 2016. I stepped out in faith and purchased my second house without help from anyone. My dad had helped by paying the down payment on my first house, and my husband had helped with some of the closing costs, but I did it all by myself the second time around. I was so proud of myself. I had to change my spending habits and become more frugal. As any homeowner can tell you, a house comes with responsibilities. When problems with my house or the yard happened, I had to make sure that I had money saved up for rainy days. As a single mom, taking care of my house became increasingly challenging, but God blessed me with the income needed to take care of my son and our home.

Around this same time, I became more comfortable sharing personal information about myself with my colleagues, but I learned the hard way that sometimes telling people about your goals, dreams, or what God has put in your heart can be discouraging. I shared my goals with a few co-workers, but they were met with negativity. One person asked, "Whom are you going to teach? What are you going teach? You are not doing anything at the moment to teach in a lecture hall." I was a quality assurance analyst at the time, performing software testing for a timeshare company. After listening to the comments, I began to question myself and started feeding into the lies. These thoughts would play over and over in my head, and I would ask myself, "Karen, who are you? Who do you think you are? You are an immigrant from Jamaica with no affluence, network, or a Harvard type of education to pursue the highest level of education." I cried. I started doubting myself. For weeks and months, I would feel less than.

Fortunately, during this time, I was getting closer and closer to God. I even decided to take another dip in the water at the church that I was attending in Las Vegas. I felt like putting on the ring one last time to show my love and dedication to Christ publicly. Again, this was not a requirement, but I did it as a personal choice that felt right. The church had me fired up for God, and I started feeling more powerful than I had ever felt before. I literally felt that I could do ALL things through Christ, who strengthens me (Philippians 4:13). I passed all of my classes and had a GPA of 3.8, but then it happened again: The devil stole my joy. In 2018, my ex-husband reached out to me in hopes of us having a better relationship. I thought that his feelings were genuine, so I indulged him. I realized a month later that he wanted a little more from me. He started joking about us having a second child together. These conversations happened over the phone as I was preparing for a trip to Jamaica. I had promised my ex-husband that our son would spend the summer holiday with him.

INSURMOUNTABLE TRIALS
AND TRIBULATIONS

M Y PLAN WAS TO STAY for 2 weeks and that he would return our son to Las Vegas after 1 month. We reconnected while I was in Jamaica on vacation and decided to give our relationship a second chance. However, before our relationship progressed, I was blindsided by the fact that he had a girlfriend. It turned out that he was in a relationship with one of the women with whom he'd had an affair while we were married. The hurt resurfaced, and I felt betrayed all over again. He asked for forgiveness and promised my son and me that he would never hurt us again; he said that he wanted his family back. I thought that God was giving our family a second chance at a life together. After flying back to the States, he informed me that his parents advised against our relationship, so we broke up, but after weighing all of the pros and cons, I still decided to move to Jamaica in August 2018 with our son. I rented my house in Las Vegas, got approval from my manager to work from Jamaica as a contractor, and shipped all of my belongings to Jamaica within 2 weeks of returning to the States.

My son was angry about the changes, but he soon accepted them and quickly became acclimated to his new environment. Even though I was born in Jamaica, moving back there still felt a little foreign to me because I had been raised in the United States for most of my life. I had to get used to my new life in Jamaica. My ex-husband came around again, wanting me to give him a third chance. Initially, I rejected the idea, but he was persistent and promised our son AGAIN that we would be a family. I reluctantly gave him this last chance, which turned out to be the worst decision that I could have made. After a short time, we broke up because he said that his parents thought that he needed time by himself before committing again. Between July and September of 2018, my ex-husband hurt me more than he did in the 10 years that we were together. While trying to move on with my life, I was propositioned by my ex-husband months after he had gone back to his girlfriend. I was disgusted! His family did not know all this information, and they did not know that he wanted me to play the side chick role that his girlfriend once played. His family disrespected me, despite knowing that I had done nothing to deserve such treatment. When I turned down his offer, he became upset and started to do things to hurt me purposefully. I could not understand why God allowed this to happen, and it eventually messed with my mental state. I was not able to complete my assignments, so I failed two classes that semester. I had to take the next semester off to get my life back on track.

I bawled and yelled at God as I remembered specifically praying and asking God to show me the way and answer whether I should move to Jamaica. I said, "If this is what you want for my life, please make everything work out seamlessly." Everything worked out seamlessly, from the request to work from Jamaica for the same company that I was employed with, to renting my house, shipping ALL my furniture and belongings to Jamaica, and starting my limited liability company. I completed all of this within 2 weeks, which was an insanely short period of time. Some people cannot pack and move within the same city, much less out of the country in 2 weeks, so I asked God why He had allowed these people to treat me like this. I was mad at God, but it was not for me to understand; God knew why He had allowed the mistreatment and betrayal. They did it, but God did it. When someone hurt you, that person carried out the act, but God made the person do it to remove that person from your life.

Weeping may last for the night, but joy comes in the morning (Psalm 30:5). After picking myself up from the floor one night after I'd had my screaming match with myself, I realized that God was not screaming back at me; instead, I felt His presence as He listened while I poured out my pain to Him in that empty house. I felt Him holding me, comforting me, and whispering that everything would work out in my favor. He told me that He loved me. I can still feel that warmth of His love, even as I type this document. Soon after, my life in Jamaica began to improve. I started to spend more time with my family members. I went out more often, and I was genuinely happy again. I found a home church in Ocho Rios and continued building my relationship with God. Eventually, I moved to Kingston in July 2019. I was doing well in all of my classes; I had to retake the courses that I had failed in 2018, but it felt good to be focused again. Life was great.

My son was preparing to start high school in September of 2019, so we travelled to the United States for back-to-school shopping. He got sick in August with a cold but felt better in the latter part of September. On the other hand, the cough that I developed toward the end of August did not ease up. My coughing got worse, and I felt weak throughout the days. September brought new symptoms: I was coughing up blood and experiencing fatigue, night sweats, fever, loss of appetite, weight loss, and shortness of breath. I had these symptoms while I was preparing to travel to Atlanta for my third and last doctoral residency. I sought medical attention: I went to several doctors and hospitals, but no one could give a definitive diagnosis. It wasn't until I went back to the emergency room in October and asked for an X-ray that I was told that I was very sick. I was referred to a pulmonologist to perform further testing.

Can you imagine the thoughts rushing through my head when I received the referral? The anxiety! I went to Dr. Google, and yes, it was scary. One of the worst things you can do when you are ill and have severe symptoms is self-diagnose on Google. I self-diagnosed using the internet, and I started to panic. I got an appointment 3 days after my ER visit. The pulmonologist requested several tests, including one for HIV. He had to order the test before performing any procedures because of my symptoms. Let me tell you, I could not function for the 3 days of waiting for the test results. I hadn't had sex in 2 years before my reconnection with my ex-husband because I was deeply invested in connecting with God and doing the things that were pleasing to Him. I had my yearly checkup with my gynecologist, but not after reconnecting with my ex-husband. Stress would be an understatement if you were to ask me how I was feeling. I finally got the good news that the HIV test result was negative, which could leave only one thing: cancer. I received the news on a Monday, and the doctor's assistant scheduled a bronchoscopy and biopsy for the following Thursday.

The results of the bronchoscopy and biopsy revealed the worst medical news: I was informed that it looked as if I had lung cancer. I was numb for days, but I had to make some decisions. I purchased a ticket to travel to Las Vegas in December for a second opinion, because the doctor had wanted to do a procedure to remove the abnormal tissue in my lungs. I wanted another set of eyes to look at my lab work. I also had to request that my doctor's office send an e-mail to my school to explain my medical condition. I was at the school's mercy because school policy states that learners will fail automatically if they do not attend the residency. I also was preparing to go to court because my ex-husband had filed for custody of our son. At the same time, I was wrestling yet again with my faith. Again, why God? I am back on track, and life is good. I am happy. My son is healthy and happy. Why am I going through so many things at the same time? Why? I am grateful that my faith in God was much bigger than a mustard seed at the time, so I kept praying and hoping for the best. My school approved my not attending the residency, so I was able to continue working toward completing the program. I also decided to move back to the United States because the pulmonologist in the States told me that based on the inconclusive results of the biopsy and the images taken during the bronchoscopy, it looked as if I had cancer and that further testing would be needed. In addition, being that my mom was my only support system, I needed to be with her and to get the care that I needed without spending all of my savings. I had so many people praying for me during this time: Family, friends, and church members prayed for me day and night. For the weapons of our warfare are not carnal but mighty in God for pulling down strongholds (2 Corinthians 10:4).

A SECOND CHANCE AT LIFE

WE MOVED BACK TO LAS Vegas in January of 2020, around the onset of the COVID-19 pandemic but before the lockdowns came into force. I had to leave all of my furniture in Jamaica because we needed to move in 3 weeks to seek medical help as soon as possible. I got insurance and started seeing another pulmonologist in the United States. Two weeks after returning, severe pain led me to the emergency room again. The doctors ordered an X-ray and told me that the cancer was spreading and that I needed to see my pulmonologist for additional care. I couldn't breathe after hearing the report. I went to my car and sat inside it for almost an hour before I was able to drive. I was crying uncontrollably, and all that I could think about was my son. I begged God for the chance to live to see my son get married and give me time with grandchildren. I thought about my paternal grandmother, who had died of lung cancer, and that made me start thinking that it was hereditary. Like my grandmother, I have never smoked a day in my life. When I finally got home, I went to his room and hugged him tightly for a few hours. I sobbed in the dark in silence.

With more testing, including another HIV test, I was diagnosed in February of 2020 with endobronchial tuberculosis (TB). Endobronchial tuberculosis is a special case of TB that relates to breathing complications. It is an infection of the tracheobronchial tree, the functional part of the respiratory system that moves air from the upper airways to the lungs. The HIV test result was negative. I was relieved to know that it was not cancer, but I also knew that I had a long road to recovery. I started taking 13 pills daily for the first month, 8 per day for the second month, and 4 per day for the last 4 months. Upon one of my visits to the TB clinic, the doctor informed me that I might have to get an airway stent implanted to help with my breathing because of the severity of my case, even after 6 months of therapy. Three months into my therapy at the TB clinic, I got laid off. I received the call the same day my son was celebrating his 13th birthday. It was hard to keep a smile on my face that day, but I had to pull through because I wanted him to have a good time. We were still in lockdown, so his friends couldn't come over, and we couldn't go to any fun places. I cried the following day: I was, sick, jobless, hurt, and feeling lost; I had tenants living in my home; and I did not know when I was going to be able to heal, move back into my home, and furnish my house again. I was broken.

I did not know it then, but God had a plan for my life, so I kept trusting in God. Though He slay me, yet will I trust in Him (Job 13:15). After 3 days of lying in bed bingeing on Netflix, I decided to focus on my schoolwork. This was my second time taking Track 3 for my residency, and I was determined to do well. Five days after being unemployed, I received a call from a recruiter at a startup company in Las Vegas. I did not think that I was qualified for the job because I had experience only with manual testing, not automated testing. I went through 3 interview rounds that same week and landed the job after 1 week. I went on to become the second QA engineer at the company. I was earning less than what I was making previously, but I was grateful for the opportunity and worked hard to learn and add value from Day 1. I was promoted to QA lead in 3 months and had five direct reports.

Things were going well financially, educationally, and mentally, and my health began to improve. I was happy once again. The devil, yes, the devil, used someone I trusted to speak nonsense to me. But then again, sometimes, we cannot blame the devil for our poor choices. The gentleman working on my estate planning at the time recommended that I work with a friend of his to eliminate some of my debt. I wanted to get rid of some of my credit cards, but my plan was going to take a long time to pay off. I reached out to his friend, and he told me to sign up for his program and that once we started the process, I should stop making payments on my credit cards. That sounded like a bad idea; every bone in my body was screaming DO NOT DO IT, but I went ahead and signed the contract. In less than 3 months, my credit scores started to go down. I panicked and told him I was done with the program; I needed to get my credit scores back up, but he said it was too late and that he was close to making agreements with the companies in question. Everything started to fall apart financially. I had never been in this situation, and I am embarrassed to even write about it, but I want to be transparent about my bad choices, the consequences of those bad choices, and what I did to get myself out of them. To add insult to injury, I had to rush to the ER again in August because I had blisters and excruciating pain on the left side of my torso. I was diagnosed with shingles. Like really? I was 40 years old! I had had chickenpox when I was a little girl, but again, I was not in my 50s or 60s. The doctor told me that it is rare to get shingles before the age of 40, but because my immune system was so weak and compromised, my body had no protection against the viral infection. I was mentally stronger at that point, so it did not affect me. I was more annoyed that I had ended my 6-month TB therapy and developed a case of shingles only 2 weeks later.

Why did I write so much about TB? Because, unfortunately, it is still stigmatized. To be honest, I was reluctant to share my diagnosis with family and friends because of this said reason, but I should not and no longer feel shame. TB is spread by someone with active TB through microscopic droplets released into the air via a cough, a sneeze, or a conversation. A person can contract TB the same way that COVID-19 could be contracted. My TB doctor told me I had had it in my system for 2 years, which explained why my case was so severe. This information helped me to trace it back to Las Vegas. Over the 2 years in question, I was a homebody: I was taking care of my son, going to the office, doing schoolwork, and attending church. The number of TB cases continue to rise, but in 2021, the World Health Organization reported that case notifications decreased because of the disruption in services caused by the pandemic. I read an article that last year, 1.5 million people died of TB. Please seek medical assistance if you are experiencing any of the aforementioned symptoms.

December 2020 rolled around, and I was promoted again to QA manager. At this time, I decided to regain control of my finances. I called all of the credit card companies to inform them that I no longer had a power of attorney and to only contact me going forward. I then reached out to a company that made credit repairs to assist me with my negotiations with the credit card companies and to help increase my credit scores. I signed a contract with the company in March of 2021, and in 1 year, my credit scores rose to a level where I was able to get a good interest rate; I was approved to buy the beautiful home that I currently reside in.

Let us get back to December 2020. It had been 4 months since I had ended the program with the TB clinic. I was preparing to take the comprehensive exam for the doctoral program in January, and I had many more work responsibilities. At this point, I decided to work on an actual vision board, not just make a list. I went into the kitchen with my cartridge paper and pen, started writing, printed images online, and completed my vision board in 2 hours.

Healing

GRACEFULLY BROKEN
BUT HEALING

THE YEAR 2021 WAS FILLED with blessings, a smidge of heartache, and healing. The new me signed up for therapy sessions in January, a choice that was a life changer. I had already been working on trying to be the best version of myself, but I never thought that I needed a therapist to help me. During my sessions, I released so much anger, resentment, heartache, disappointments, failures, rejection, defeat, and regrets. I had forgiven my ex-husband in 2014 for all of the hurt that he had caused me, but when I went back to him in 2018, he hurt me even more. I forgave him again, but this time, I released everything. I forgave his family for mistreating and disrespecting me, I forgave my father for hurting me a few times in the past, and I forgave myself for the things that I kept beating myself up about.

Love yourself, know your worth, and teach people how you want to be treated. Letting go of things or people that no longer serve you is okay. It may hurt for some time, but your life will be better without the things that are draining you. The thief comes only to steal, kill, and destroy; God has come so that you may have life and have it more abundantly (John 10:10). People come into your life for a reason, a season, and a lifetime. Use discernment for spiritual guidance, and when you feel it in your spirit, let go, move on, be obedient, and do it. Rejection is protection. Pray for those who have wronged you, and do not try to seek revenge. God is your vindicator; allow Him to work on your behalf. The healed version of me allows me to be my authentic self; radiate love, compassion, forgiveness, happiness, and peace; and truly live out my purpose in life.

God was certainly healing me, but I also needed to put in some work with my therapist to heal fully. As mentioned previously, healing allowed me to live a life of peace and joy that I had never experienced before. However, the peace did not last long because the road to my doctoral degree stopped when I was told that I could not continue with my dissertation topic. After working on this topic for almost 2 years, my former mentor told me that he would not be able to approve my topic because no one was going to sign up for my study. The topic was too new and advanced. He did not believe in me. He did not try to help me whatsoever. He made this announcement during the 4th week of the semester. I had 6 weeks to find a new topic, get it approved, and get all of the previously completed milestones completed again. I was awaiting my presentation with my research committee members on Milestone 6 to get research approval and complete Milestone 7. What my former mentor requested of me was impossible! He knew, but he did not care. He took pleasure in failing me. The program states that if a student receive two non-satisfactory grades while working on a dissertation, it is an automatic failure, and the learner is removed from the program.

I was crushed. I questioned God again. Why are You allowing this to happen to me? I have been through too much! Make it stop! When will I ever get a break?! I took the following semester off to figure out what I wanted out of life and find my purpose. After 2 months of praying, searching my heart, and engaging in self-reflection, it came back to one thing: teaching. I decided to go back to school and complete what I had started in 2016, even if I had to research a completely new topic. I was off to a good start with a new mentor in 2022 and a new topic. I worked closely with two of my committee members on the new topic and got to a point where I was able to get it approved. However, when I got my new topic approved, I was informed that I could resume work on my old topic with some minor changes. I almost lost it! But after crying and seeking God, I did not ask any questions. I knew that there must have been a reason why God delayed my getting committee approval of my original topic, so I thanked Him. One year after I was told that I could not work on my original topic, it was approved by my new committee members, who raved about it enthusiastically.

Therapy also helped me to end a toxic relationship with a narcissist after 2 years of dating. Therapy helped me to be a more present mom to my son. After what I went through with my son's father and then getting sick, losing my job, dealing with the college, and messing up my finances, I realized that I wasn't there for him as much as I used to be. He needed me at this time because it was hard for him, too. He had endured a lot of hurt and disappointment. To add to his pain, he had to relocate 3 times in 2 years and had to stay home for 1 year because of COVID-19. I eventually signed him up for therapy because I did not want him carrying around resentment and anger and one day taking it out on the people who loved him the most. Through my illness and therapy, I also had a relationship with my father that was the best that we'd had in a long time. I am happy that he is back in my life, and I am grateful for the quality time that we have spent with each other since 2021.

THE RIGHT OPPORTUNITIES

IN JANUARY 2022, I WAS promoted to QA director. My salary was now double that of my starting salary. I dropped to my knees and cried when the promotion was announced. I thanked God for making all of this possible. I thanked Him for humbling me throughout the last few years. I prayed that He would continue to have favor on my life and my son's life. I prayed for His protection, guidance, support, grace, and blessings. My son and I are destined for greatness, something that I remind him of all the time. Life brings challenges, but we must hold onto our faith and know that storms always produce great miracles.

After my promotion in January, I got approved for my home loan in February, sold my house in March, closed on my newly built house in July, flew to Jamaica with my mom and son to spend 2 weeks in one of the most beautiful hotels in Ocho Rios, Jamaica, and moved into our new home in August with all new furniture. I was on Cloud Nine. I was singing God's praises from the mountaintop. Nothing could stop my momentum. My life was full of joy, blessings, and abundance.

Fast forward to October 4, 2022. I went in for surgery, a procedure that I had been delaying for a year. I was on medical leave for 3 weeks. Upon returning to work, I was laid off the same day around 9:00 a.m. PDT. It came as a shock, but then again, maybe not. I had seen the writing on the wall the week before I went on medical leave. I was sad but relieved. I had worked in that toxic environment for a little more than 2 years. I had wanted to leave for the longest time, but I had never had the courage to do so. I had become complacent, so God removed me from that workplace. However, I will be grateful forever for the opportunity that the company gave me. I can use everything that I learned at that company in the classroom. I know that everything happens for a reason.

I WILL LIFT UP MY EYES
UNTO THE HILLS

I HAVE BEEN UNEMPLOYED FOR 2 months, but I keep the faith that God has something better in store for me. The battle is not mine; it belongs to God (2 Chronicles 20:15). Despite my circumstances, I have peace, love, and joy in my life, and I feel blessed. God is working everything out in my favor, and now, I am getting ready to ring in the new year. 2023 is going to be EPIC! I have a new vision board. I achieved all but two things on my old vision board. I am more active in my new church home. I am grounded, stronger than ever before, courageous, and unstoppable. I will complete my doctoral program in 2023 and become a professor. This is what God has planned for my life, and I know that it will come to pass. The road to greatness is not easy: It is not for the faint of heart, but it is worth it if you persevere.

What would have happened if I had not been obedient when God told me to pack my things immediately after returning from Las Vegas? The pulmonologist had confirmed that the biopsy results looked like cancer, so who knows what would have happened to me? If I hadn't moved back to Las Vegas in January 2020, I would have stayed in Jamaica and allowed my former pulmonologist to remove the abnormal areas from my lungs. I did not have cancer; I had endobronchial TB, so who knows what the outcome of unnecessary surgery might have been? I lost my job in April of 2020. Who knows how long I would have been unemployed if I had stayed in Jamaica?

Given that the world was on lockdown, so many people were unemployed, and I was living outside of the States; eventually, I probably would have had to move in with family members because of my financial difficulties at the time. I also would have had to go to court to battle my ex-husband over custody of our son. I was prepared for the legal challenge because I had one of the best attorneys in Kingston, but my health and job status would have become an issue over time. How would I have overcome those problems if I had stayed in Jamaica? I wouldn't have. God made sure that my TB had the same symptoms as lung cancer. He made sure that the doctor misdiagnosed me so that I could return to Las Vegas, where He wanted me, and He also made sure that I moved before the lockdown. No one knew in January 2020 that COVID-19 would shut down the world! When I think about this in my alone time, I am amazed by the goodness of God. I am now where I am supposed to be, and I couldn't be happier.

God has given me double for my trouble. My son and I live in a beautiful home, and we are extremely happy and healthy. My mom is with us all the time, so she is practically a resident, too. Haha. I was blessed with an opportunity to work for a company that allowed me to grow and trusted me to be one of the leaders to help contribute to the company's growth and meet its business objectives. Plus, I am creating generational wealth for my family. I have been investing for more than 2 years, something that I tried to do on and off for 10 years but could not because whenever I saved my money and tried to invest, I had to use it for emergencies. Over the last 4 years, I have grown mentally, emotionally, and spiritually. While going through all of my trials and tribulations between 2018 and 2021, I did not imagine having the life I have now, which is why I believe that sometimes God must break you to prosper you.

Never give up on yourself, and never give up on your future. Always believe in yourself, and keep the faith, even if your faith is as small as a mustard seed. Whatever God planted in your heart when you were a child or a young adult, hold on to it. I have learned that when I put God first, He puts me first, and I've learned that I should never fear the enemy because God will never leave nor forsake me (Deuteronomy 31:8). The first thing that I do in the morning is spend my alone time with God. My morning routine has helped me over the last 6 years. This may work only for some of you, but it has worked for me. Almost every morning, I have to say "almost" because life happens, I pray, read Bible scriptures, meditate on God's word or guided meditation, journal, say affirmations, and exercise. I read the Miracle Morning by Hal Elrod this year, and it confirmed what I have been doing all of these years.

You may ask, "What do I do if I don't know my purpose?" I suggest that you explore your passion. Ask yourself what you're passionate about and what makes you happy when you are doing that thing. Once you think about the thing that makes you happy, you still might tell yourself that following that passion will not make sense financially, so think again. Don't do something just in pursuit of money; instead, allow God to develop you into the person that He created you to be. Once you do that, the money will come. Develop good habits, and focus on solutions, not problems. Whatever your purpose may be, if you follow that path, God will ensure that you achieve your dreams. Trust Him. Go after your dreams, and do not second-guess yourself. You have everything you need to fulfill your destiny. God gave you the talent that you need to become great.

When I pray, I remind God that He said that with long life, He will satisfy me and that because I delight myself in Him, He will give me the desires of my heart. My latter days will be greater than my former days. God will be with me, just as He was with Moses. I may not know what the future holds, but I trust God enough to lead me while I continue to follow Him. Sometimes, it may look impossible, but I know that God can do the impossible. I also have learned not to be angry with the people who hurt me. Not forgiving others means giving my power away, so I have to forgive them to take back my power. Forgiving them does not mean that I am okay with what they did to hurt me, but it has freed me. God gave me authority, and I refuse to allow anyone or anything to take that away from me.

Thirty-eight years after my initial dream of wanting to become a teacher, why do I still want to pursue my passion? Because this is the gift that God has given me. It still resonates with me, and I want to help others. Whenever I teach or explain something to other people and it increases their understanding, I can see their faces light up. It gives me pure joy to know that I can help others. I also want to make a positive impact on people's lives. I want to be in an environment where I can make a real difference in the lives of adult learners. By connecting to adult students' interests and diverse life skills and experiences, I can provide them with new and authentic real-world tasks. I want to be an influential professor who can create learning experiences to help adult learners to develop a passion for the subject matter. God has equipped me for this task, and I am ready to give back.

God is shaping me to assume my purpose and destiny. I hope that you allow God to work in you and for you. Yes, the road to greatness is rocky, but believe in yourself. There is purpose to your pain, so do not allow your pain to hinder or delay what God has planned for your life.

We are all human, so it is fine to have moments that involve venting, crying, yelling, and taking a break, but we cannot let those fleeting moments turn into weeks, months, or years. God controls your seasons, so have comfort in knowing that your bad seasons are temporary only. Be strong and courageous, for you shall cause this people to inherit the land which I swore to their fathers to give them (Joshua 1:6). The mind is a battlefield, so take control of your mind, and don't allow the wrong people and their negativity into your life. If you think that you cannot, you probably will not. Surround yourself with positive people who are going to add value to your life. If you don't have positive people in your life just now, remember that having God is more than enough. I have been through a lot of ups and downs in my life, and I have experienced many challenges and hardships. I have overcome past challenges and obstacles, and I continue to pursue my goals and passions. I turned to my faith and relied on God to guide me through difficult times. As I move forward, I will continue to find strength and support in my faith. Love yourself, and keep going.

Protection

Whoever dwells in the shelter of the Most High
will rest in the shadow of the Almighty.
I will say of the Lord,
"He is my refuge and my fortress, my God, in whom I trust."
He will cover you with His feathers,
and under His wings you will find refuge;
His faithfulness will be your shield and rampart.
For He will command His angels concerning you
to guard you in all your ways;
they will lift you up in their hands,
so that you will not strike your foot against a stone.
With long life I will satisfy him and show him my salvation.

Psalm 91:1-2, 4, 11, 16

@kcoombs2023/

Love Yourself and Keep Going Book

@ karen-coombs-053100a/

@loveyourselfandkeepgoing

www.ingramcontent.com/pod-product-compliance
Lightning Source LLC
Chambersburg PA
CBHW040859120626
46551CB00001B/84

* 9 7 8 1 9 5 5 6 2 2 2 9 5 *